THE BOOK I

For all of humanity

THE BOOK I

For all of humanity

Ramanamma Who?

Illustrations by Kalpart

Strategic Book Publishing and Rights Co.

Book Design/Layout, Illustrations and Book Cover design by Kalpart.
Visit www.kalpart.com

Strategic Book Publishing and Rights Co., LLC
USA | Singapore
www.sbpra.net

For information about special discounts for bulk purchases, please contact Strategic Book Publishing and Rights Co., LLC. Special Sales, at bookorder@sbpra.net.

ISBN: 978-1-68235-288-5

All of Humanity

The Appointed Time

We each of us have an appointment that we will keep without fail. This appointment was not made *by* us but was made *for* us by our creator. It is where we are all going and cannot be avoided. We do not know when or where this appointment will be, but that will not matter. We will keep this appointment no matter what we do, where go, or how far we travel in life. When we attend this appointment, this will be the last thing, on earth, we will ever do. If you have not figured it out yet, "the appointment" I am referring to is the moment of your death.

Western society, in particular, does not like to talk about this subject and in fact goes a long way to persuade people not to think about it, claiming it is not healthy or it is morbid to dwell on such matters. Yet every single one of us, young, old, male or female, will reach this point *without* fail. Some sooner than others and in a variety of forms and manners. No matter how rich or poor, good or bad a person you have been, death *is* the great equalizer.

In case you are thinking that this book is going to be full of doom and gloom, I can assure you that this book is exactly the opposite. My purpose in writing it is to show you that rather than being the end, which we all believe it to be, "the appointment" is in fact the whole purpose of us being here in the first place.

In the time it has taken me to type these paragraphs, approximately 12,000 babies have been born worldwide. Another way to look at it is 12,000 appointments have been made, and perhaps as many as 10,000 people, again worldwide, have kept their appointments (or died).

Now the vast majority of us never think about this appointment, and yet you do have one. You will not be late and, contrary to popular belief, you will not arrive earlier than expected. You will arrive exactly as scheduled, not a minute too soon.

You may have asked yourself from time to time "What is the purpose of life?" or "Why are we all here?" While it may not be a very satisfying answer, "the appointment" is exactly the reason any of us are here. You can argue that appointments seem to be random happenstances, but you cannot argue that you yourself will have one of these randomly circumstanced appointed times.

The Peace of God

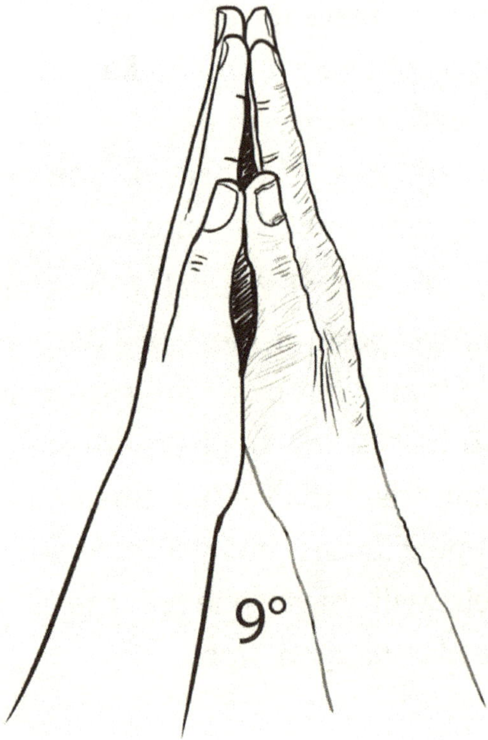

Someone asked me the question, "What kind of peace would you like?" and I answered, "The peace of God that passes all understanding." My response confounded the asker. The answer appears paradoxical in that we imagine the peace of God cannot be understood and, therefore, beyond the reach of humanity. When looked at carefully, what is actually being said is that God's peace, when you have it, passes understanding. A simpler way to say it is this: understanding is not necessary to obtain the peace of God.

Language, useful as it is, is severely limiting when it comes to describing things that pass all understanding. This is because when we talk about such matters as God's peace, we have to go beyond the boundaries of the material realm, and our vocal utterings lack the capacity to articulate anything it cannot comprehend. Language, while pretty limited in the answers department, fairs a bit better when it comes to forming questions. Language is a pretty good enquiring tool, especially on a material level.

I want to explain a bit more what it means by passing understanding. It simply means it cannot be grasped by the mind. There is another way, however, to glimpse and then fully immerse yourself in the parts of existence that pass understanding, namely the peace of God.

"What is that way?" I hear you ask. Well, the good news is you are already in it, have always been in it, and will never not be in it. There are variations that say the same thing and all are paradoxical. A paradox has a cancelling effect, meaning that anything that is a paradox is immediately cancelled out. But wait, I am not answering your question directly. I will waste no more time trying to explain what can't be explained but hope it has helped you to see why; it couldn't be explained..

So how do you enter the peace of God? Suspend belief and invest in knowing when belief is no longer required then knowing becomes the predominate driving force, and this knowing is where the peace of God resides.

Actions in knowing are decisive, clear, and executed with accuracy 100 percent of the time. Actions in belief can be indecisive, unclear, and can be hit and miss. The hits can become knowing but can also just continue to be a belief. Now before I get accused of being a "beliefist" (another new word) against belief, let me clarify the difference between belief and knowing. Belief is like continuing to drive around in your old unreliable car when you could be driving in the ultimate car. The ultimate car, or knowing, will never let you down and can take you places you have never been before, which you could never have gotten to in your old "beliefist" model. What I am saying is this: a belief is something you think it is, whereas a knowing is certain and beyond thought. No thinking is required.

Take the things you believe and convert them into knowing. This way, beliefs will either be discarded when untrue, or those that turn out to be true become knowing and no longer require thought.

The Day

There has only ever been one day and this is it. You are in it. A twenty-four-hour day consists of daylight and nighttime. The sun and the moon have always appeared in a loop and fluctuate according to the seasons, which also gives us temperature changes. These are in the same and only day there has ever been. Perception and observation give the illusion that there has ever been more than this day. Our perceptions and observations give names to the slight changes that occur during the sun and moon exchange, names such as Monday or Tuesday, ten o'clock or nine p.m., cold or warm, dentist appointment or visit to the zoo. During our perceptions of time, as we seemingly move through the day, we observe and perceive objects and the slight changes as we sense the day. As the things we observe, or are aware of, change, we imagine that the day has changed, but this is not the case. The day has not gone anywhere; it is the same day it has always been. What has changed is our perception of it. It is claimed that billions of days have gone before us, but this is just an illusion. There is only one day and this is it.

If you have read and understood what you have read, then you will know that there has only ever been one day. Why is this significant? Well, if many days are an illusion, what else is an illusion in this day? The closer we look—through microscopes or telescopes—the less anything appears as it seems. Is it all an illusion? I think we can agree that our perception of the day changes constantly but consists largely of the same things: sunrise, noon, evening, sleep, wakefulness, jobs, rest, etc. During the course of the day, or perceived lifetime, other perceivers will appear and disappear and we will interact with them; these are tentacles from the same source—tentacles of perception and observation from different perspectives. Everything is perceived as experience, and experience is just the shading or colouring of perceived changes of the day. All that is required for anything to exist is one day. This day, the same day, that you have been experiencing as a multitude is, in fact, singular and has only ever been one.

This is a different perspective on what has been shown to be a simple truth: everything appears in and from one source. Separateness and multitude are just an illusion brought about by perception and observation. If I take the two concepts of perception and observation and blend them, we get consciousness or awareness. If we take those two concepts and do the same, we get knowing. All there is, is the knowing of the day.

We'd like to know if you enjoyed the book. Please consider leaving a review on the platform from which you purchased the book

CPSIA information can be obtained
at www.ICGtesting.com
Printed in the USA
LVHW040205161022
730798LV00025B/762

9 781682 352885